The Legend
of
Rami the Wolf

Elizabeth U. Stanley

Illustration by Eric Gonzales

The Legend of Rami the Wolf

Copyright © 2016 by Elizabeth U. Stanley

ISBN 13:
Paperback: 978-1-68256-592-6
PDF: 978-1-68256-593-3
ePub: 978-1-68256-594-0
Kindle: 978-1-68256-595-7

Printed in the United States of America.

LitFire
PUBLISHING
LitFire LLC
1-800-511-9787
www.litfirepublishing.com
order@litfirepublishing.com

Dedication

The Legend of Rami the Wolf is dedicated to the memory of Rami; a very special wolf.
1993 – 2008

Howling Rami
Photo: Annie White

My name is Rami. I am a fourteen year old gray wolf. I am not a very big wolf; only about seventy-five pounds. My home is the Mission: Wolf Sanctuary in the Southern Rocky Mountains of Colorado.

Rami
Photo: Monty Sloan/wolfphotography.com

Wolf Raven was my mother. She, her sister Jordan, and her brother Lucus used to live on a dairy farm in Wisconsin. They were happy at the farm but it just wasn't a good place for wolves to live. As young pups they were allowed to run free on the farm. Sometimes they enjoyed milk treats directly from the cows.

Raven
Photo: Tracy Ane Brooks

2

Though it seemed rather harmless to see the cute pups frolic around the farm with the other animals and children, a neighbor became concerned. Those pups would grow to be wolves with instincts that did not belong on a farm. Irresponsible care would surely prove to be harmful to the wolves as they became adults.

The neighbor knew of a refuge called Mission: Wolf Sanctuary in Colorado. A friend of Mission: Wolf learned of the pups and placed a call to the refuge where the founders agreed to accept one of the young wolves. With the intent of rescuing only one of the pups, upon meeting the young wolves they kindly brought all three of them to live at the refuge.

Remote Mission: Wolf Sanctuary
Photo: Elizabeth U Stanley

Mission: Wolf was a very special place for rescued captive wolves that could not survive in the wild. There, the wolves had plenty of food and water, and most of all, lots of room to run. They were much happier living with other wolves and the kind people who cared for them. Raven became the alpha wolf of her pack. With her were her sister Jordan, also known as Snaggletooth, and her brother Lucus.

Raven's Pack – Raven, Jordan, Lucus and Nikkolah
Photo:Tracy Ane Brooks

Mission: Wolf was home to several other wolves. One day Nikkolah, a wolf from another pack, sneaked out of his enclosure. He was a very smart wolf. He figured out a way to get through the fence and into Raven's enclosure with her pack. He and Raven became mates and before long, Nikkolah became my father. The people at the refuge called him "Tricky Nicky." He joined Raven's pack and with my brothers and sister, we were a family.

Nikkolah
Photo: Tracy Ane Brooks

Besides my family of wolves, I was very fortunate also to have a special friend. His name was Tamas and he was like a brother to me. Somehow we had a special bond and way of understanding each other. Tamas took care of me and we had our own special ways of talking to each other. We were together much of the time and really enjoyed each other's company as we played or just hung-out together. It was fun having a people-brother. Tamas made me feel special and we cared very much for each other.

There were many large enclosures for other wolves at Mission: Wolf. Each wolf was rescued from a place where it was unhappy, unwanted, or even abused. At Mission: Wolf wolves were respected and loved. There, each pack could live together in a natural wooded area surrounded by open space and forest. There were high places on hills and in the rocks where a wolf could stand and look far across the landscape of wild country. At Mission: Wolf the wolves could feel safe and protected.

Room to run and high places to climb
Photo: Tracy Ane Brooks

Raven was her pack's alpha wolf for a long time. Wolves know when it is time for a new leader, and Raven was getting old. Her sister Jordan helped my sister Nyati challenge our mother to take over as the alpha wolf. Nyati won the challenge and Raven left the pack to live in her own enclosure. That is the way of the wolf.

Nyati
Photo: Tracy Ane Brooks

My life has been good at Mission: Wolf. There I have met so many people who have come to the refuge to learn about wolves. Because I am not afraid of people and have a friendly disposition, I have been allowed to greet people at the sanctuary. I have had opportunities to travel around the country and teach others about wolves. Few wolves have been where I have been. Let me tell you about my very special life.

Rami greeting visitors at the sanctuary
Photo: Tracy Ane Brooks

As a pup I enjoyed playing with my brothers and sister. We felt very secure in our home and the people at Mission: Wolf were very good to us. Sometimes we would run and run until we reached the tall fence that went around our special space. As I sat at the fence, looking out over the mountains and valleys that seemed to go on forever, I could not help but wonder. What would it be like to run with the pack to the far away valley? What would it be like to see an elk herd and to learn to hunt to feed the pack? What would it be like to follow the raven or to be free like the eagle?

Our mother taught us many things, but we could never be free. We were captive-born wolves that could not survive in the wild. But we were among the fortunate wolves that were given a home where we could live our lives with care and respect from people who believed in our dream that one day all wolves would be free.

A safe home with care and respect
Photo: Maxine U Woolsey

Somehow I was a special wolf. As I grew older, the people at Mission: Wolf taught me about trust and being trusted. We had great respect for each other. They taught me to walk with them with a collar around my neck and a long leash so I could explore. They took me for a ride in a big bus with a special place inside just for me to live while on the long tours to teach people about us.

They were teaching me to be an Ambassador Wolf. Very few wolves have that honor. I was so proud. I could not be free, but I could teach people about wolves so one day all wolves could be free. My life had a purpose, and I did my very best to encourage protection for my kind and to make a brighter future for all wolves to live free in the wilderness.

Proud Rami
Photo: Nelson Brooke

After being an Ambassador Wolf for a while, greeting people who visited the refuge, it was my turn to travel across the country in the big bus to meet people who needed to know more about wolves so they wouldn't fear them. People are often afraid of things they don't understand.

Ambassador Wolves Sila and Merlin were retiring and I was to take their place. It was so exciting and I hoped I could do the same good job that Sila and Merlin had done. Little did I realize the adventures that were in store for me. I was beginning a lifetime of service that would prove to be more than any other wolf had done for the survival of our species.

Ambassador Wolves Sila and Merlin
Photo: Tracy Ane Brooks

Mission: Wolf's Kent, Tracy and sometimes Tamas arranged for our tours and the many stops we would make along the way to teach people about wolves. The bus would be packed with everything that would be needed for our long adventure. When it was time to leave the refuge I said goodbye to my pack mates and boarded the bus with my people companions. Jumping up onto the platform in my special section of the bus, I could watch out the window as the refuge disappeared in the distance as we drove away. It was so exciting.

After riding for a while the world began to look very different than it did at the sanctuary. There were so many things to see as I sat looking out my window as we drove across the country. Sometimes the world seemed very confusing with horns blowing, cars racing by, and big tall buildings everywhere. So many people seemed to be in such a hurry. At those times I felt safe in my bus with my friends Kent and Tracy.

And sometimes there were scents in the air that I had never smelled before; scents my big nose did not understand. The pollution from cars and factories near the cities smelled very different from the clean fresh smells in the forest.

There were other times that out my window I could see open fields and meadows, green forests with glistening waterfalls and streams, rolling hills and tall mountains. During those times my nose enjoyed the more familiar smells of fresh air and meadows. To stretch my legs, sometimes Kent would stop the bus and take me for a walk through a wooded area or by a lake where I could swim. In my heart I felt such a longing to be with my pack, running wild and free through the forest. But that was not to be for me. My life had another purpose; a very special purpose.

We would be away from the refuge for about a month on these tours. The special space for me on the bus was to be my home during that time. When it was dark and I curled up on my bed for the night, I dreamed that I lived in a beautiful wilderness. In my dreams, the pack taught me the ways of the wolf. They taught me respect, loyalty, trust, survival skills, and to be wise. My dreams took me to a world that I would never see. Somehow I had been chosen to show the world about how important wolves are to the balance of nature, and how they must be protected. Mission: Wolf gave me that chance.

As we traveled from state to state many of our stops were at schools. Children from kindergarten through high school were given a chance to see a live wolf and to gaze into my beautiful yellow eyes. When I came through the door there was silence in the room. Even the squirmiest of children became still and all were in awe of me. I felt very important. And indeed I was important.

Yellow eyes of a wolf
Photo: Jessica Stanley

Through me, Kent and Tracy would teach people about wolves and how we are needed to complete nature's balance. They would teach them to respect wolves and to tell others about what they had learned. After all, as these children grow up, they are the ones who will be our educators and protectors.

Wolf Education Program
Photo: : Elizabeth U. tStanley

Day after day we made public appearances. Every time it was the same. Seeing a live, majestic wolf entering a room seemed always to command respect from the audience. People from all walks of life would have a chance to see the wolf very differently than they had before. My ability to interact with people was very unique as wolves are usually very shy of people. Through me people could learn the ways of the wolf and that we only want to live our lives free in the wild.

Wolf behavior
Photo: Elizabeth U. Stanley

As Tracy walked me around the room, Kent would talk to the people and tell them about wolf behaviors. Sometimes he would hold a treat high in the air to show my strength by how high I could jump. Once in a while I would stop in front of someone and greet him eye-to-eye. People asked questions and there were flashes from cameras.

Rami jumps to show her strength
Photo: Elizabeth U. Stanley

Many attitudes about wolves have been changed once people have heard the real stories and had the opportunity to meet eye-to-eye with a gray wolf. Kent asked the people to share their pictures and what they had learned so others could understand the wolf in a good way. It always felt good to greet people and to know that many of them would become advocates for us because I was there.

Up close with nature
Photo: Elizabeth U. Stanley

There was an exciting tour to Idaho and the Pacific Northwest one year. It was to the 13th Annual Wolf Conference, and I was to be a guest. As luck would have it, an air line on the bus broke moments before I was to appear on the program. Help came, and I jumped into the cab of the pick-up truck, with my people in the back, rode two miles to the conference and arrived on time. How exciting was that?

On another tour I had a chance to run in the sand along the Oregon Pacific coast. And I walked along wooded trails of cool mosses and ferns and beside mineral pools in the forest of the Cascade Mountains. For a time, I could pretend I was a wild wolf in the wilderness of my dreams.

One of my proudest moments was greeting the U.S. Senate to ask them to continue to protect wolves with the Endangered Species Act. Sessions in Congress can be rather boisterous as issues are debated among the Senators. But as I entered the room, those important dignitaries all became silent, just like the school children had done. It was my job to convince them that the wolf was worthy to be protected as it reestablished its rightful place in the ecosystem of the United States.

As Kent told his stories and made a plea to the group, I walked around proudly and on my best behavior as I knew that I represented all wolves. Those lawmakers had never experienced a wolf in such a close environment. They were amazed. I think I did my job well and had some influence by the fact that wolves continued to be listed at that time.

Wolves are worthy to be protected
Photo: Monty Sloan / wolfphotography.com

My story with my friend Tamas has been told in "National Geographic." I have appeared on numerous television programs; "Mr. Rogers" being one. My travels have taken me to the Grand Canyon and other notable places. I have howled to the flute with Levi Holt of the Nez Perce Native American Tribe.

Native Americans respect the wolf
Photo: Tracy Ane Brooks

I have wet my paws in both the Atlantic and Pacific Oceans. I have met thousands of people across this country in so many different places and situations. Having a purpose in my life has kept me going for all these many years. I am told that my presence has done more for wolf education and preservation than any other single wolf. Though my life has not been one of freedom, I am proud of my contribution to the public understanding and protection of my species.

Rami teaches about wolves
Monty Sloan / wolfphotography.com

There came a time when two wolf pups were rescued and brought to the Mission: Wolf Sanctuary. They were put into my enclosure for me to raise as my own. Their names were Raven, like my mother, and Magpie, sometimes called Maggie. Now I was an alpha wolf with my own pack. They were Ambassador Wolves in training. I taught them everything I knew and the next year they went with me on tour. Luna, a wolf-dog cross, went with us. Raven and Magpie did their jobs well and I knew they could carry on without me, as I was getting older and the rigorous tours were tiring.

Raven II and Magpie
Photo: Elizabeth U. Stanley

When the time came for another tour, I stayed at the refuge. It was time for me to retire. I remembered both the excitement of leaving for a new adventure each year and the joy of seeing the refuge in the distance as we drove up the hill coming home.   There was a feeling of sadness as I watched the bus roll away that time without me.

Home in the distance
Photo: Elizabeth U. Stanley

Now I am very old for a wolf, and am told that I am "aging elegantly." As I rest in a warm and peaceful place at the sanctuary, my thoughts go back to my life over the past many years. Though not completely free, few places would have given me the freedom that Mission: Wolf has made possible. Unlike many other captive wolves, I have not lived in a cage nor been confined to a small enclosure. I am very grateful to those who have devoted their lives to the rescue and protection of captive wolves.

Rami "aging elegantly"
Photo: Tracy Ane Brooks

And I am proud of my life as an Ambassador Wolf. I have had the chance to meet thousands of people, face to face, in over thirty states across the country to make a difference for my kind. From the west coast to the east coast and states in between, I became a very well-traveled wolf. In one publication, "The Sound Report" 10.19.01, I was called "the smallest wolf with the largest territory in history." When I close my eyes to dream for the last time, it will be that all wolves are free in the wilderness as they are born to be.

Photography Credits

Tracy Ane Brooks
Monty Sloan / wolfphotography.com
Nelson Brooke
Annie White
Maxine Upson Woolsey
Elizabeth Upson Stanley
Nancy Upson
Jessica Stanley

Technical Advice and Photoshop Expertise
Jeffrey Kollbrunner / JKNatureGallery.com

Inspiration
Ambassador Wolf Rami / Mission: Wolf Sanctuary, Colorado
Kent Weber and Tracy Ane Brooks / Cofounders Mission: Wolf Sanctuary

Ambassador Wolf Rami
Photo: Nelson Brooke

The Legend of Rami the Wolf

The story of Rami was written with love in the hope of my continued ability over time to contribute to the preservation of wolves in our wildernesses for future generations. My experiences with wolves have shown me that, as with all wildlife, wolves have an important role to play in the balance of an ecosystem. We can learn much from the wolf. As stewards of this planet, maybe one day people will learn to co-exist in harmony with nature's creatures.

Elizabeth U. Stanley

A portion of the profits from the sale of <u>The Legend of Rami the Wolf</u> will be donated to wolf rescue and recovery.

Rami Howls for Harmony
Photo: Annie White

CPSIA information can be obtained
at www.ICGtesting.com
Printed in the USA
BVOW07s1550080916
461363BV00008B/74/P